# Miracles on Maple Hill

## Novel Literature Unit Study and Lapbook

Unit Study Created by Teresa Ives Lilly

www.hshighlights.com

This unit can be used in any grade level in which students are able to read the book. The activities are best used in grades 2 to 6. Almost everything in the unit can be used to create a file folder lap book. Each unit study covers one whole book and includes:

**Comprehension Activities:**
   Fill in the Blanks, True and False, Multiple Choice,
   Who, What, Where, When, Why and How Questions.

**Pre-Reading Skills Activities**
   Author Information Activity, Time line Activity, Theater Box Activity

**Lesson Activities**
   Encyclopedia, Journal, Vocabulary, Sequence of Events, Handwriting
   Main Idea, Key Event, Prediction, Comparison,

**Literature Skills Activity**
   Main Character, Main Setting, Main Problem, Possible Solutions, Character Traits, Character Interaction, Cause and Effect, Description, Pyramid of Importance, Villain vs. Hero

**Poetry Skills Activity**
   Couplet, Triplet, Quinzain, Haiku, Cinquain, Tanka, Diamanté, Lantern and Shape Poem

**Newspaper Writing Activity**
   Editorial, Travel, Advice Column, Comics, Society News, Sports, Obituary, Weddings, Book Review, Wanted Ads, Word Search

**Creative Writing Activity**
   Letter, Fairy Tale, Mystery, Science Fiction, Fable, Dream or Nightmare, Tall Tale, Memoir, Newberry Award, A Different Ending.

**Writing Skills Activity**
   Description, Expository, Dialogue, Process, Point of View, Persuasion, Compare and Contrast, Sequel, Climax and Plot Analysis.

**Poster Board Activity**
   Collage, Theater Poster, Wanted Poster, Coat of Arms, Story Quilt, Chalk Art, Silhouette, Board Game Construction, Door Sign, Jeopardy.

**Art Expression Activity**
   Main Character, Main Setting, Travel Brochure, Postal Stamp, Book Cover, Menu, Fashion Designer, Puzzle, Mini Book, Ten Commandments.

**Creative Art Activity**
   Sculpture, Shadow Box, Mosaic, Mobile, Acrostic, Tapestry, Paper Dolls, Book Mark, Photography, Parade Float, Sketch

**Other Activities:**
   Sign Language Vocabulary, Literature Web, Bingo.

# Published at www.hshighlights.com
# Copyright © 2009 All rights reserved
# Teachers may make copies for their individual students only

**How to do the Lapbook Activity:** To use this unit study either print out all the pages or Student wills recreate most of them in a notebook or on white or colored paper.

All of the pages can be added to the lapbook project as shown in the photos, or only use those items you want to have students create a lapbook and have them use a spiral notebook for the other pages.

The following are photos of how the work can be presented in the lapbook format. To create the lapbook use 3-6 file folders (colored are best), construction paper or index cards, markers, glue and a stapler.

Front                                                                 Back

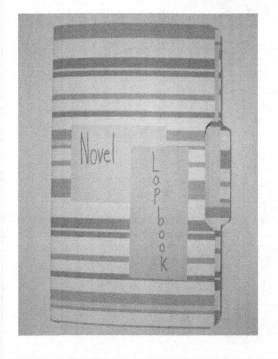

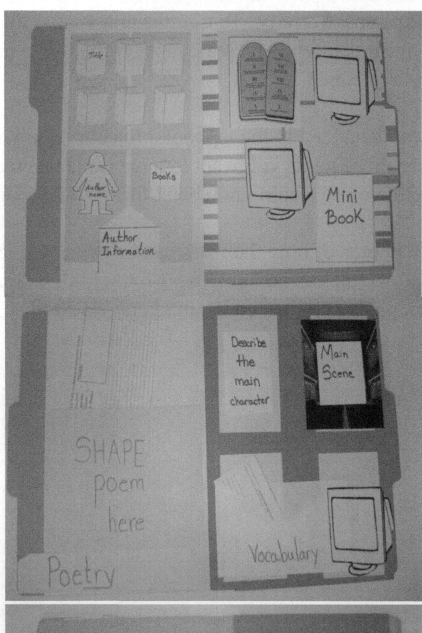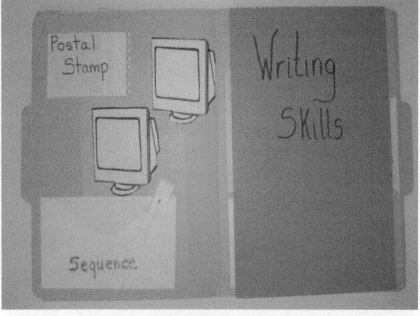

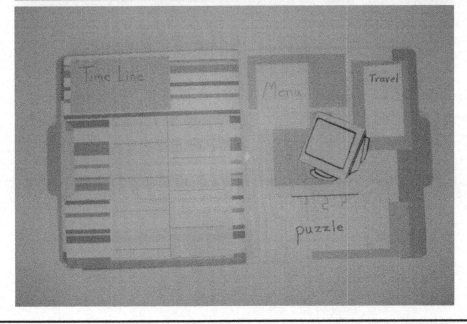

**How to do the Newspaper Activity:** As the student completes the news paper activities, have student lay the completed work out on a big board or on several poster boards. Don't have them glue the items on the board until the entire newspaper is completed and all sections are put where the student wants them to be. Have student create a name for their newspaper. Then have them type out the name, in big bold letters and place it on the top of the board. with tape or sticky clay. Then tape of stick all the completed articles onto board as well.

# Pre-Reading Activities

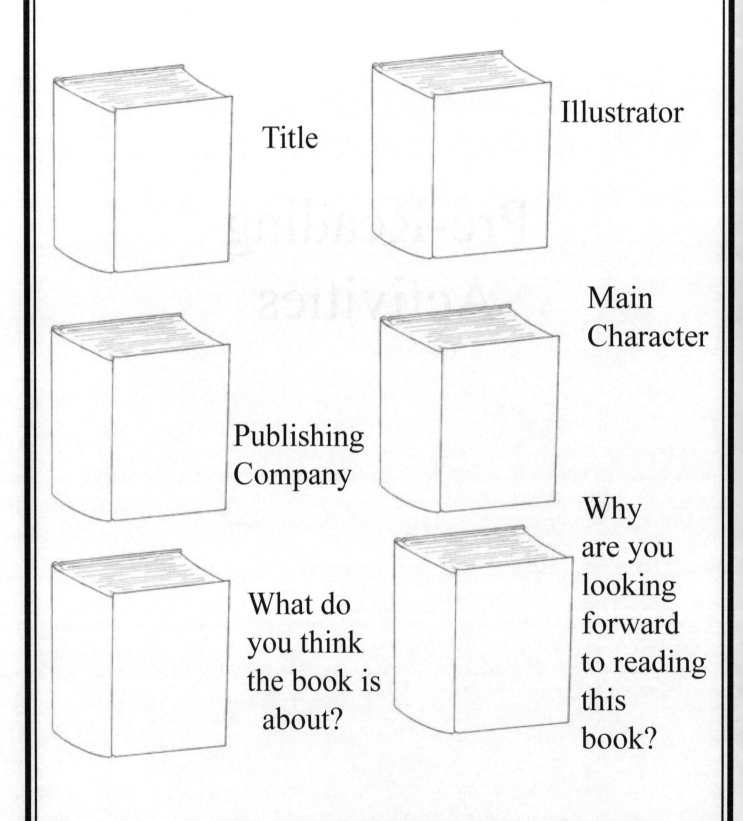

**Author Activity:** Student will use the book they are studying and information found on the internet to find out information about the author. Then student will write the information required for this activity on the patterns or in their notebook. The patterns may be cut out and placed on the lapbook.

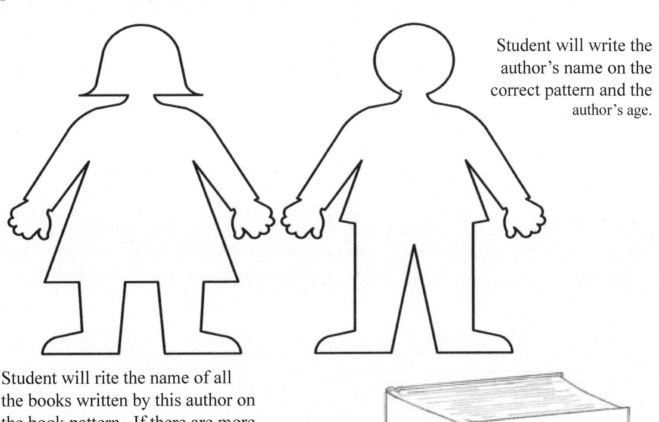

Student will write the author's name on the correct pattern and the author's age.

Student will rite the name of all the books written by this author on the book pattern. If there are more than three books, just select the three most famous.

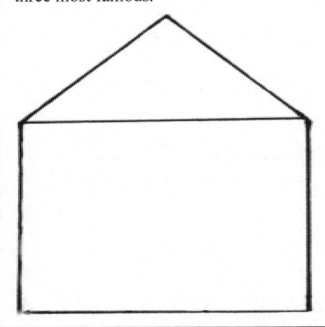

Student will write information about the author on the house pattern, such as where the author was born, lived and how they became an author.

**Time Line Activity:** Student will use the book they are studying to fill out the time line indicating when anything new, interesting or important happens in the book. This time line pattern can be copied into the student's notebook or this pattern can be printed smaller and placed on the lapbook.

All Vocabulary Lists, Comprehension Questions, True and False, Fill in the Blank for each lesson are at the end of this unit study.

# Lesson 1
# Activities

**Lesson 1 Activities:** Students will use the book they are studying and information found on the internet for the following activities. Then the student will write the information required for this activity on the patterns or in their notebook. The patterns may be cut out and placed on the lapbook.

**Encyclopedia:**
Student will choose one subject from this lesson that interested them and look it up on the internet or in encyclopedia. They will write the name of the subject across the top of the monitor pattern. On the monitor screen section, they will write three or more interesting facts about the subject.

**Journal:**
Student will imagine that they are one of the characters from the story. After reading each lesson, they will write a short journal entry telling what happened from that character's point of view.
Student will also draw a picture to go along with the journal entry.
At the end of the book, student will staple all the journal entries together to form a complete booklet.
They can even create a special cover for it from construction paper.

Vocabulary word: _____
Definition of the word: _____
_____
_____

Antonym of the word: _____
How many syllables does the word have? _____

Vocabulary Word: _____
Sentence using the word: _____
_____
_____

Synonym of the word: _____

**Vocabulary:** Student will use the vocabulary words from the list for this lesson. On one of the patterns, or on one index card they will write one vocabulary word. They should also write the definition of the word, then the Antonym and how many Syllables the word has.

On the other card, the student will write the same word. They will write a full sentence using this word and then write the Synonym of the word.

They will repeat this for all the vocabulary words in this lesson.

Place the patterns or cards in an envelope which can be glued into the student's notebook or onto the lapbook..

**Sequencing:** At the end of the lesson the student will write two of the main events on these two strips. Save them in an envelope which can be glued onto the lapbook or in the notebook. At the end of the book, these strips can be taken out and the student can arrange them in the correct order as they occurred in the story.

**Handwriting:** Student will pick their favorite sentence that they read in this lesson. Have them write the sentence in their best handwriting on this page or in their notebook.

**Student will write out the answers for the following:**

**Main Idea:** In a sentence or two, write what the main idea was of this section.

_____
_____
_____
_____
_____
_____

**Key Event:** In a sentence or two write what the most important event was in this section.

_____
_____
_____
_____
_____
_____

**Prediction:** In a sentence of two write what you Predict will happen in the next section.

_____
_____
_____
_____
_____
_____

**Comparison:** In a sentence of two compare two things in this section. Tell what makes them alike and what makes them different.

_____
_____
_____
_____
_____
_____

**Fact or Opinion:** In one sentence write a fact about this section and one sentence that is an opinion about the lesson.

_____
_____
_____
_____
_____
_____

**Literature Skills: Main Character:** Student will write words in the circles to describe the main character.

Physical appearance

Concern or worry

Main character

Who they relate to

Your opinion of them

**Poetry Form:** Student will write a poem about the book or characters using this format.
**Couplet:** A Couplet is a two line poem with a fun and simple rhyming pattern. Each line has the same number of syllables and their endings must rhyme with one another. Humor is often used in couplets.

Example:
If a seed could have its way
it would grow in just one day.

_____
- - - - - - - - - - - - - - - - - - - - - - - - - - - - - - -
_____
_____
- - - - - - - - - - - - - - - - - - - - - - - - - - - - - - -
_____
_____
- - - - - - - - - - - - - - - - - - - - - - - - - - - - - - -
_____
_____
- - - - - - - - - - - - - - - - - - - - - - - - - - - - - - -
_____

**Newspaper Activity:** Student will use this form to write their newspaper piece on then paste it onto their newspaper lay out poster.

**Editorial:** An editorial is written by the editor of the newspaper. In an editorial the editor gives an opinion of something. Student will imagine that they are the editor of their newspaper. Student will write their opinion of something that happened in the book so far.

# Editorial

**Creative Writing Activity:** Student will use this form or write in their notebook.
**Letter Writing:** Student will write a letter from one character in the book to another character in the book.

Dear          ,

Sincerely,

**Writing Skills Activity:** Student will use this form or write in their notebook.

**Descriptive**: Descriptive writing uses words such as color and texture to describe something. Student will describe a person, place or thing from the lesson.

**Lapbook Activity: Main Character:** Student will draw and color a picture of the main character on the solid section of the flap book. Student will cut out the entire flap book on the dotted lines and fold the four flap sections over the picture of the main character. On the outside of each flap student will write different words that describes the character; one word per flap.

## Poster Board Activity:
**Book Collage**
Student will print out pictures from the internet that represent characters from the story. They can use magazine pictures as well. Then student will glue these pictures all over a 1/2 poster board in an over lapping fashion to create a book collage.

## Creative Art Activity:
**Sculpting**
Student will create on of the characters from the story out of clay or play doe.

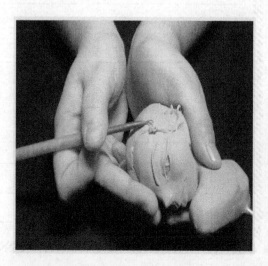

# Lesson 2
# Activities

**Lesson 2 Activities:** Students will use the book they are studying and information found on the internet for the following activities. Then the student will write the information required for this activity on the patterns or in their notebook. The patterns may be cut out and placed on the lapbook.

**Encyclopedia:**
Student will choose one subject from this lesson that interested them and look it up on the internet or in encyclopedia. They will write the name of the subject across the top of the monitor pattern. On the monitor screen section, they will write three or more interesting facts about the subject.

**Journal:**
Student will imagine that they are one of the characters from the story. After reading each lesson, they will write a short journal entry telling what happened from that character's point of view.
Student will also draw a picture to go along with the journal entry.
At the end of the book, student will staple all the journal entries together to form a complete booklet.
They can even create a special cover for it from construction paper.

Vocabulary word: _____
Definition of the word: _____
_____
_____

Antonym of the word: _____
How many syllables does the word have? _____

Vocabulary Word: _____
Sentence using the word: _____
_____
_____

Synonym of the word: _____

**Vocabulary:** Student will use the vocabulary words from the list for this lesson. On one of the patterns, or on one index card they will write one vocabulary word. They should also write the definition of the word, then the Antonym and how many Syllables the word has.

On the other card, the student will write the same word. They will write a full sentence using this word and then write the Synonym of the word.

They will repeat this for all the vocabulary words in this lesson.

Place the patterns or cards in an envelope which can be glued into the student's notebook or onto the lapbook..

**Sequencing:** At the end of the lesson the student will write two of the main events on these two strips. Save them in an envelope which can be glued onto the lapbook or in the notebook. At the end of the book, these strips can be taken out and the student can arrange them in the correct order as they occurred in the story.

**Handwriting:** Student will pick their favorite sentence that they read in this lesson. Have them write the sentence in their best handwriting on this page or in their notebook.

**Student will write out the answers for the following:**
**Main Idea**: In a sentence or two, write what the main idea was of this section.
_____
_____
_____
_____
_____
_____

**Key Event:** In a sentence or two write what the most important event was in this section.
_____
_____
_____
_____
_____
_____

**Prediction:** In a sentence of two write what you Predict will happen in the next section.
_____
_____
_____
_____
_____
_____

**Comparison:** In a sentence of two compare two things in this section. Tell what makes them alike and what makes them different.
_____
_____
_____
_____
_____
_____

**Fact or Opinion:** In one sentence write a fact about this section and one sentence that is an opinion about the lesson.
_____
_____
_____
_____
_____
_____

**Main Setting:** Student will fill in the information to describe the main setting and to describe the minor settings in the story.

What is the main setting? _____
_____

Describe it _____
_____
_____
_____

Describe a Minor Setting
_____
_____
_____

Describe a Minor Setting
_____
_____
_____

**Poetry Form:** Student will write a poem about the book or characters using this format.

**Triplet:**
Triplets are three-lined poems that rhyme. Each line has the same number of Syllables.

Example:
    The bunny hops and hops
    Til all at once she stops
    To munch some carrot tops.

_____
_____
_____
_____
_____

**Newspaper Activity:** Student will use this form to write their newspaper piece on then paste it onto their newspaper lay out poster.

**Travel Section:** Student should imagine they write the travel column for a newspaper. Student should write a short article about traveling to the area where this book takes place. Student should find one or two photos on the internet that reminds them of this place and place it on the newspaper lay out poster as well.

# Travel

**Creative Writing Activity:** Student will use this form or write in their notebook.

**Fairy Tales** : Fairy Tales are fanciful tales of legendary deeds and creatures, usually intended for children. Student will write a fairy tale involving one of the characters from the story and illustrate it.

**Writing Skills Activity:** Student will use this form or write in their notebook.

**Persuasion**: Persuasion is a way of writing, in which you convince someone of something. Student will write to try to persuade someone in the story to do something differently than they did in the story.

**Lapbook Activity:** **Main Setting** : Student will draw and color the main scene or main setting of this story for a play in this stage scene. Place in lapbook.

**Poster Board Activity:**
**Theater Poster**
Student will create a poster that may be found outside of a theater which is putting on a play of this book.

**Creative Art Activity:**
**Shadow Box:**
Student will use a shoe box turned on its side to create a scene from the book in using pictures from the internet or other small items.

# Lesson 3
# Activities

**Lesson 3 Activities:** Students will use the book they are studying and information found on the internet for the following activities. Then the student will write the information required for this activity on the patterns or in their notebook. The patterns may be cut out and placed on the lapbook.

**Encyclopedia:**
Student will choose one subject from this lesson that interested them and look it up on the internet or in encyclopedia. They will write the name of the subject across the top of the monitor pattern. On the monitor screen section, they will write three or more interesting facts about the subject.

**Journal:**
Student will imagine that they are one of the characters from the story. After reading each lesson, they will write a short journal entry telling what happened from that character's point of view.
Student will also draw a picture to go along with the journal entry.
At the end of the book, student will staple all the journal entries together to form a complete booklet.
They can even create a special cover for it from construction paper.

Vocabulary word: _____
Definition of the word: _____
_____
_____

Antonym of the word: _____
How many syllables does the word have? _____

Vocabulary Word: _____
Sentence using the word: _____
_____
_____

Synonym of the word: _____

**Vocabulary:** Student will use the vocabulary words from the list for this lesson. On one of the patterns, or on one index card they will write one vocabulary word. They should also write the definition of the word, then the Antonym and how many Syllables the word has.

On the other card, the student will write the same word. They will write a full sentence using this word and then write the Synonym of the word.

They will repeat this for all the vocabulary words in this lesson.

Place the patterns or cards in an envelope which can be glued into the student's notebook or onto the lapbook..

**Sequencing:** At the end of the lesson the student will write two of the main events on these two strips. Save them in an envelope which can be glued onto the lapbook or in the notebook. At the end of the book, these strips can be taken out and the student can arrange them in the correct order as they occurred in the story.

**Handwriting:** Student will pick their favorite sentence that they read in this lesson. Have them write the sentence in their best handwriting on this page or in their notebook.

**Student will write out the answers for the following:**

**Main Idea**: In a sentence or two, write what the main idea was of this section.

_____
_____
_____
_____
_____

**Key Event:** In a sentence or two write what the most important event was in this section.

_____
_____
_____
_____
_____

**Prediction:** In a sentence of two write what you Predict will happen in the next section.

_____
_____
_____
_____
_____

**Comparison:** In a sentence of two compare two things in this section. Tell what makes them alike and what makes them different.

_____
_____
_____
_____
_____

**Fact or Opinion:** In one sentence write a fact about this section and one sentence that is an opinion about the lesson.

_____
_____
_____
_____
_____

**Main Problem:** Most stories seem to have one main problem. There may be other small problems, but there is an overall large problem. Student will write what the main problem is in the larger rectangle, and some of the smaller problems in the smaller ones.

**Poetry Form:** Student will write a poem about the book or characters using this format.

**Quinzain:** Quinzains are unrhymed three line poems that contain 15 syllables. The pattern is: The first line is 7, the second is 5 and the third is 3. The first line makes a statement and the next two lines ask a question about the subject.

Example:
  I like to write poetry
  would you like to write
  a poem too?

**Newspaper Activity:** Student will use this form to write their newspaper piece on then paste it onto their newspaper lay out poster.

**Wanted Ads Section:** Student will create several wanted ads that characters in the story might post in a newspaper or ads the characters might answer.

# Wanted Ad

# Wanted Ad

# Wanted Ad

# Wanted Ad

**Creative Writing Activity:** Student will use this form or write in their notebook.

**Mystery:** Student will write a mystery that may occur in this story or to the characters in this story and then illustrate it.

**Writing Skills Activity:** Student will use this form or write in their notebook.

**Expository:** Expository writing is writing strictly to inform. Student will write an expository piece that informs someone about an event that happened in the story.

**Lapbook Activity: Travel Brochure:** Student will use this form to create a travel brochure on. It should describe a place in the story that people should come to visit. Student may use pictures from the internet if necessary.

## Poster Board Activity:
**Wanted Poster**
Student will create a "Wanted by the Law," poster for one of the villains in the story.

## Creative Art Activity:
**Mosaic Plate**
Student will create a mosaic scene from the story on a paper plate using small pieces of construction paper glued in a mosaic fashion.

# Lesson 4
# Activities

**Lesson 4 Activities:** Students will use the book they are studying and information found on the internet for the following activities. Then the student will write the information required for this activity on the patterns or in their notebook. The patterns may be cut out and placed on the lapbook.

**Encyclopedia:**
Student will choose one subject from this lesson that interested them and look it up on the internet or in encyclopedia. They will write the name of the subject across the top of the monitor pattern. On the monitor screen section, they will write three or more interesting facts about the subject.

**Journal:**
Student will imagine that they are one of the characters from the story. After reading each lesson, they will write a short journal entry telling what happened from that character's point of view.
Student will also draw a picture to go along with the journal entry.
At the end of the book, student will staple all the journal entries together to form a complete booklet.
They can even create a special cover for it from construction paper.

Vocabulary word: _____
Definition of the word: _____
_____
_____

Antonym of the word: _____
How many syllables does the word have? _____

Vocabulary Word: _____
Sentence using the word: _____
_____
_____

Synonym of the word: _____

**Vocabulary:** Student will use the vocabulary words from the list for this lesson. On one of the patterns, or on one index card they will write one vocabulary word. They should also write the definition of the word, then the Antonym and how many Syllables the word has.

On the other card, the student will write the same word. They will write a full sentence using this word and then write the Synonym of the word.

They will repeat this for all the vocabulary words in this lesson.

Place the patterns or cards in an envelope which can be glued into the student's notebook or onto the lapbook..

**Sequencing:** At the end of the lesson the student will write two of the main events on these two strips. Save them in an envelope which can be glued onto the lapbook or in the notebook. At the end of the book, these strips can be taken out and the student can arrange them in the correct order as they occurred in the story.

**Handwriting:** Student will pick their favorite sentence that they read in this lesson. Have them write the sentence in their best handwriting on this page or in their notebook.

**Student will write out the answers for the following:**
**Main Idea**: In a sentence or two, write what the main idea was of this section.
_____
_____
_____
_____
_____

**Key Event:** In a sentence or two write what the most important event was in this section.
_____
_____
_____
_____
_____

**Prediction:** In a sentence of two write what you Predict will happen in the next section.
_____
_____
_____
_____
_____

**Comparison:** In a sentence of two compare two things in this section. Tell what makes them alike and what makes them different.
_____
_____
_____
_____
_____

**Fact or Opinion:** In one sentence write a fact about this section and one sentence that is an opinion about the lesson.
_____
_____
_____
_____
_____

**Possible Solutions:** Problems in a story can have several solutions. Student will write what some of the problems are in the story and possible solution in the shapes.

Problem:

Solution:

Problem:

Solution:

Problem:

Solution:

**Poetry Form:** Student will write a poem about the book or characters using this format.

**Haiku:** A haiku is a Japanese poem with no rhyme. Haiku poems have only three lines, each with a certain number of syllables.
Here is the pattern:
Line 1 = 5 syllables
Line 2 = 7 syllables
Line 3 = 5 syllables

Example:
Lion cubs doze in
shade, under shrubs, hidden from
hungry hyenas

**Newspaper Activity:** Student will use this form to write their newspaper piece on then paste it onto their newspaper lay out poster.

**Advice Column Section:** Student will come up with a question or concern that one of the characters in the story may have. The student will write a letter to the advice column and the advice column writer will answer.

# Advice Column

**Creative Writing Activity:** Student will use this form or write in their notebook.

**Science Fiction:** Science Fiction stories take place in the far future usually in space or on earth in an advanced society. Student will write a science fiction story about the future of one of the characters and illustrate it.

# Writing Skills Activity: Student will use this form or write in their notebook.

**Dialogue**: A dialogue is a conversation between two characters. Student will write a dialogue that could occur between two characters in the story. Student should use correct quotation marks.

**Lapbook Activity: Postal Stamp:** Student will create a new postal stamp for next year which would represent the book or characters of the book.

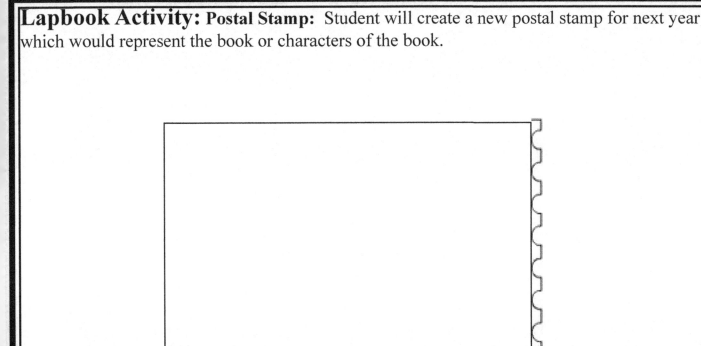

## Poster Board Activity:
### Coat of Arms
Using a poster board, student will create a coat of arms with a design to represent this story or a character in the story.

## Creative Art Activity:
### Mobile
Student will cut out pictures from the internet of characters of items that represent those in the book and then glue them onto long strips of card board. These can be hung with string to make a mobile.

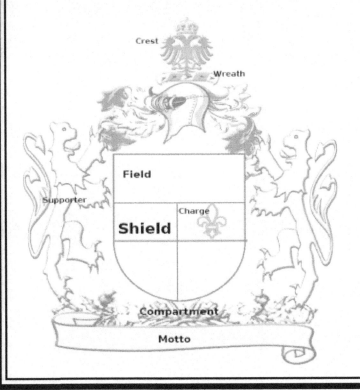
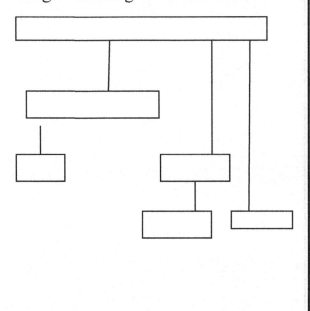

# Lesson 5
# Activities

**Lesson 5 Activities:** Students will use the book they are studying and information found on the internet for the following activities. Then the student will write the information required for this activity on the patterns or in their notebook. The patterns may be cut out and placed on the lapbook.

**Encyclopedia:**
Student will choose one subject from this lesson that interested them and look it up on the internet or in encyclopedia. They will write the name of the subject across the top of the monitor pattern. On the monitor screen section, they will write three or more interesting facts about the subject.

**Journal:**
Student will imagine that they are one of the characters from the story. After reading each lesson, they will write a short journal entry telling what happened from that character's point of view.
Student will also draw a picture to go along with the journal entry.
At the end of the book, student will staple all the journal entries together to form a complete booklet.
They can even create a special cover for it from construction paper.

Vocabulary word: _____
Definition of the word: _____
_____
_____

Antonym of the word: _____
How many syllables does the word have? _____

Vocabulary Word: _____
Sentence using the word: _____
_____
_____

Synonym of the word: _____

_____
_____
_____
_____
_____
_____

**Vocabulary:** Student will use the vocabulary words from the list for this lesson. On one of the patterns, or on one index card they will write one vocabulary word. They should also write the definition of the word, then the Antonym and how many Syllables the word has.

On the other card, the student will write the same word. They will write a full sentence using this word and then write the Synonym of the word.

They will repeat this for all the vocabulary words in this lesson.

Place the patterns or cards in an envelope which can be glued into the student's notebook or onto the lapbook..

**Sequencing:** At the end of the lesson the student will write two of the main events on these two strips. Save them in an envelope which can be glued onto the lapbook or in the notebook. At the end of the book, these strips can be taken out and the student can arrange them in the correct order as they occurred in the story.

**Handwriting:** Student will pick their favorite sentence that they read in this lesson. Have them write the sentence in their best handwriting on this page or in their notebook.

**Student will write out the answers for the following:**

**Main Idea**: In a sentence or two, write what the main idea was of this section.
_____
_____
_____
_____
_____
_____

**Key Event:** In a sentence or two write what the most important event was in this section.
_____
_____
_____
_____
_____
_____

**Prediction:** In a sentence of two write what you Predict will happen in the next section.
_____
_____
_____
_____
_____
_____

**Comparison:** In a sentence of two compare two things in this section. Tell what makes them alike and what makes them different.
_____
_____
_____
_____
_____
_____

**Fact or Opinion:** In one sentence write a fact about this section and one sentence that is an opinion about the lesson.
_____
_____
_____
_____
_____
_____

**Character Traits:** In the circle for the Main Character Traits, student will write several of the main character's traits. In the circle for Student Traits, student will write several of the student's traits. Any traits that the main character and the student have in common should be in the area where the circles overlap called Common Traits.

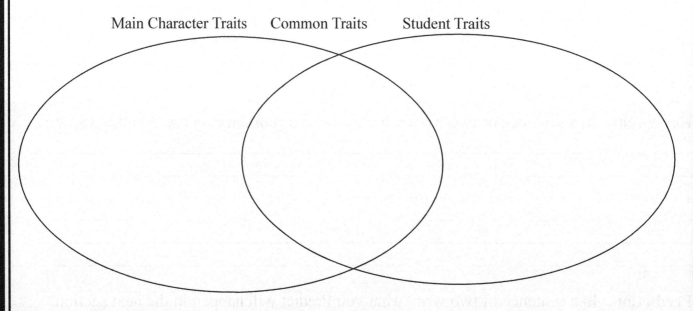

**Poetry Form:** Student will write a poem about the book or characters using this format.

**Acrostic:** In an acrostic poem the name of the person, object, or place is written vertically down the left hand side of the page. Each letter is capitalized and becomes the first letter of the word beginning each line. The words used should describe the person, object or place in a positive way. Each line may comprise a word, a phrase or a thought that is continued on to the next line.

Example:
CAT
Can you see their eyes
At night in the dark
They glow........

_____
_____
_____
_____
_____
_____
_____
_____
_____
_____

**Newspaper Activity:** Student will use this form to write their newspaper piece on then paste it onto their newspaper lay out poster.

**Comic Section:** Student will create a funny cartoon about one of the events of characters in the story. Illustrate and color it.

# Comics

**Creative Writing Activity:** Student will use this form or write in their notebook.
**Fable:** A fable is a short, allegorical narrative, making a moral point, traditionally by means of animal characters that speak and act like humans. Student will write a fable that comes to mind while reading this story in which one of the characters from the book learns a moral from an animal. Then student will illustrate it.

**Writing Skills Activity:** Student will use this form or write in their notebook.

**Process:** Process writing is telling the actual steps it takes to do something. Student will write a step by step process that one of the characters in the book had to do to or should have done.

**Lapbook Activity: Book Cover Illustrator:** Student will create their own book cover for this story on the form. Make sure to include the title, illustrator and publisher's name.

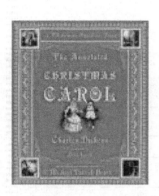

## Poster Board Activity:
**Story Quilt**
Divide a poster board into eight to sixteen equal squares. In each square the student will draw different pictures to tell what has happened in the story so far.

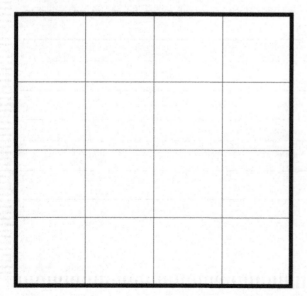

## Creative Art Activity:
**Tapestry**
Using an 8 inch by 12 inch piece of felt as the background, student will cut out characters and items from the story from colored felt and glue onto the background to create a story tapestry.

# Lesson 6
# Activities

**Lesson 6 Activities:** Students will use the book they are studying and information found on the internet for the following activities. Then the student will write the information required for this activity on the patterns or in their notebook. The patterns may be cut out and placed on the lapbook.

**Encyclopedia:**
Student will choose one subject from this lesson that interested them and look it up on the internet or in encyclopedia. They will write the name of the subject across the top of the monitor pattern. On the monitor screen section, they will write three or more interesting facts about the subject.

**Journal:**
Student will imagine that they are one of the characters from the story. After reading each lesson, they will write a short journal entry telling what happened from that character's point of view.
Student will also draw a picture to go along with the journal entry.
At the end of the book, student will staple all the journal entries together to form a complete booklet.
They can even create a special cover for it from construction paper.

Vocabulary word: _____
Definition of the word: _____
_____
_____

Antonym of the word: _____
How many syllables does the word have? _____

Vocabulary Word: _____
Sentence using the word: _____
_____
_____

Synonym of the word: _____

**Vocabulary:** Student will use the vocabulary words from the list for this lesson. On one of the patterns, or on one index card they will write one vocabulary word. They should also write the definition of the word, then the Antonym and how many Syllables the word has.

On the other card, the student will write the same word. They will write a full sentence using this word and then write the Synonym of the word.

They will repeat this for all the vocabulary words in this lesson.

Place the patterns or cards in an envelope which can be glued into the student's notebook or onto the lapbook..

**Sequencing:** At the end of the lesson the student will write two of the main events on these two strips. Save them in an envelope which can be glued onto the lapbook or in the notebook. At the end of the book, these strips can be taken out and the student can arrange them in the correct order as they occurred in the story.

_____
_____
_____
_____
_____
_____

**Handwriting:** Student will pick their favorite sentence they read in this lesson. Have them write the sentence in their best handwriting on this page or in their notebook.

**Student will write out the answers for the following:**

**Main Idea:** In a sentence or two, write what the main idea was of this section.
_____
_____
_____
_____
_____
_____

**Key Event:** In a sentence or two write what the most important event was in this section.
_____
_____
_____
_____
_____
_____

**Prediction:** In a sentence of two write what you Predict will happen in the next section.
_____
_____
_____
_____
_____
_____

**Comparison:** In a sentence of two compare two things in this section. Tell what makes them alike and what makes them different.
_____
_____
_____
_____
_____
_____

**Fact or Opinion:** In one sentence write a fact about this section and one sentence that is an opinion about the lesson.
_____
_____
_____
_____
_____
_____

**Character Interaction:** In the circles, student will write the names of the characters in the story and then draw arrows from each circle to other circles to represent which character interact with one another. Start with the Main Character in the center.

**Poetry Form:** Student will write a poem about the book or characters using this format.

**Cinquain**: A cinquain is a short, five-line, non rhyming poem which follows the following pattern:

First line - The title (one word)
2nd line - Describes the title (two words)
3rd line - Express action (three words)
4th line - A feeling or thought (four words)
5th line - A Synonym or close word for the title

Example:
Insect
six legs
usually have wings
a mostly helpful annoyance
Bee

**Newspaper Activity:** Student will use this form to write their newspaper piece on then paste it onto their newspaper lay out poster.

**Obituary Section:** Student will imagine that one or more of the characters in the book died and will write an obituary telling how they died.

**Wedding Announcement Section:** Student will imagine that one of the characters in the story will get married soon and will write the wedding announcement, telling who they will marry, where and when the wedding will take place.

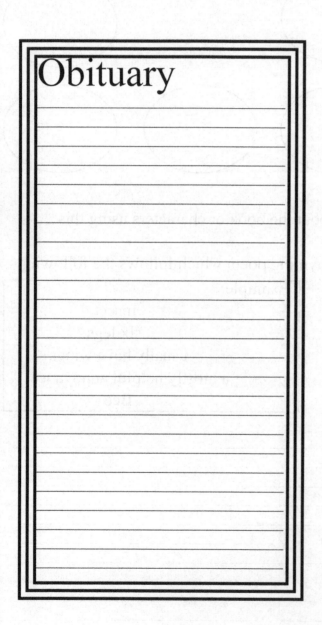
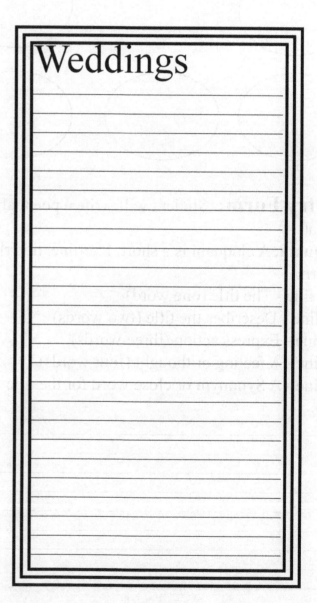

# Creative Writing Activity: Dream or Nightmare: Student will write a dream or nightmare one of the characters in the story may have, and illustrate it.

**Writing Skills Activity:** Student will use this form or write in their notebook.

**Point of View**: Point of View is telling a story from one person's view. Student will write about an event in this story from a different character's point of view.

**Writing Skills Activity:** Student will use this form or write in their notebook.

**Lapbook Activity: Menu:** Student will create a menu for a restaurant that the characters in the book may have owned or eaten at. Student will decorate the front of the menu in an interesting and inviting fashion.

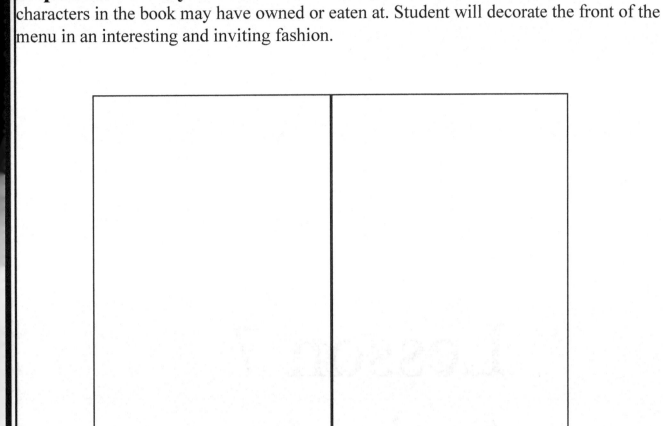

## Poster Board Activity:
**Chalk Art**
On a black poster board student will use colored chalk to illustrate a scene or event in the story.

## Creative Art Activity:
**Paper Doll**
Student will cut out pictures from the internet of people to represent the characters in this story and then laminate them and glue them onto sticks. Students can use them to act out parts of the story or the dialogue the student wrote in an earlier lesson.

# Lesson 7
# Activities

**Lesson 7 Activities:** Students will use the book they are studying and information found on the internet for the following activities. Then the student will write the information required for this activity on the patterns or in their notebook. The patterns may be cut out and placed on the lapbook.

**Encyclopedia:**
Student will choose one subject from this lesson that interested them and look it up on the internet or in encyclopedia. They will write the name of the subject across the top of the monitor pattern. On the monitor screen section, they will write three or more interesting facts about the subject.

**Journal:**
Student will imagine that they are one of the characters from the story. After reading each lesson, they will write a short journal entry telling what happened from that character's point of view.
Student will also draw a picture to go along with the journal entry.
At the end of the book, student will staple all the journal entries together to form a complete booklet.
They can even create a special cover for it from construction paper.

Vocabulary word: _____
Definition of the word: _____
_____
_____

Antonym of the word: _____
How many syllables does the word have? _____

Vocabulary Word: _____
Sentence using the word: _____
_____
_____

Synonym of the word: _____

**Vocabulary:** Student will use the vocabulary words from the list for this lesson. On one of the patterns, or on one index card they will write one vocabulary word. They should also write the definition of the word, then the Antonym and how many Syllables the word has.

On the other card, the student will write the same word. They will write a full sentence using this word and then write the Synonym of the word.

They will repeat this for all the vocabulary words in this lesson.

Place the patterns or cards in an envelope which can be glued into the student's notebook or onto the lapbook..

**Sequencing:** At the end of the lesson the student will write two of the main events on these two strips. Save them in an envelope which can be glued onto the lapbook or in the notebook. At the end of the book, these strips can be taken out and the student can arrange them in the correct order as they occurred in the story.

_____
_____
_____
_____
_____
_____

**Handwriting:** Student will pick their favorite sentence that they read in this lesson. Have them write the sentence in their best handwriting on this page or in their notebook.

**Student will write out the answers for the following:**
**Main Idea**: In a sentence or two, write what the main idea was of this section.

_____
_____
_____
_____
_____
_____

**Key Event:** In a sentence or two write what the most important event was in this section.

_____
_____
_____
_____
_____
_____

**Prediction:** In a sentence of two write what you Predict will happen in the next section.

_____
_____
_____
_____
_____
_____

**Comparison:** In a sentence of two compare two things in this section. Tell what makes them alike and what makes them different.

_____
_____
_____
_____
_____
_____

**Fact or Opinion:** In one sentence write a fact about this section and one sentence that is an opinion about the lesson.

_____
_____
_____
_____
_____

**Cause and Effect:** When one thing happens in a story, many other things happen because of this one event. This is called cause and effect. In the center circle, student will write one thing that happened in the story (the cause). In the smaller circles, student will write the variety of things that happened because of that main cause (the effects).

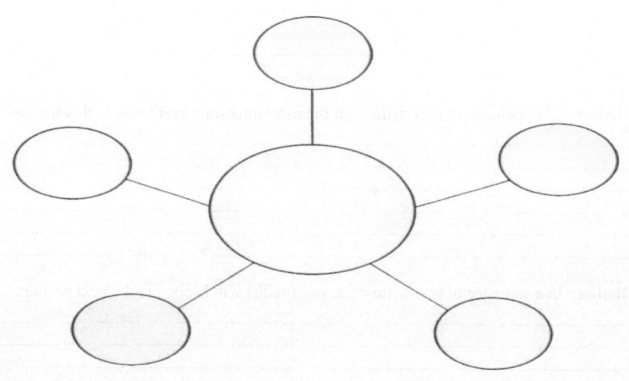

**Poetry Form:** Student will write a poem about the book or characters using this format.

**Tanka:** A Tanka is a form of Japanese poetry that depends on the number of lines and syllables instead of rhyme. The pattern is:
Line 1 = 5 syllables,  Line 2 = 7 syllables
Line 3 = 5 syllables,  Line 4 = 7 syllables
Line 5 = 7 syllables

Example:
Blue-eyed baby cubs
wobble out of winter's den
warm sun on cold fur
forest smells of fresh, cold pine
wild, new world to grow into.

**Newspaper Activity:** Student will use this form to write their newspaper piece on then paste it onto their newspaper lay out poster.

**Society News Section:** Student will write about someone in the story who would be considered a fairly famous person or character. Write a society column about an event or party that they may have attended.

**Creative Writing Activity: Tall Tale**s: Tall tales are humorous, exaggerated stories common on the American frontier. Student will write a tall tale about one of the characters in the story and then illustrate it.

**Writing Skills Activity:** Student will use this form or write in their notebook.

**Compare and Contrast**: Compare and Contrast tell about two or more things and how they are alike or different. Student will write to Compare and Contrast two characters in the story.

**Lapbook Activity: Fashion Designer:** Student will design clothing that one or more of the characters in the story would have worn. Student will color them or cut them out of scraps of material and put them on the doll form that represents the character and then attach to lapbook.

## Poster Board Activity:
### Silhouette
Using black construction paper, student will cut out a silhouette of the main character or an item from the story and glue it onto the center of a white or colored 1/2 poster board. Then student will create a frame around the outside with a black poster board.

## Creative Art Activity:
### Book Mark
Using thick tag board, student will cut into a rectangle 3 inches by 6 inches, and create a book mark that resembles something about the book. Then student will punch a hole in the end and tie ribbon or string through it. Laminate it if possible.

# Lesson 8
# Activities

**Lesson 8 Activities:** Students will use the book they are studying and information found on the internet for the following activities. Then the student will write the information required for this activity on the patterns or in their notebook. The patterns may be cut out and placed on the lapbook.

**Encyclopedia:**
Student will choose one subject from this lesson that interested them and look it up on the internet or in encyclopedia. They will write the name of the subject across the top of the monitor pattern. On the monitor screen section, they will write three or more interesting facts about the subject.

**Journal:**
Student will imagine that they are one of the characters from the story. After reading each lesson, they will write a short journal entry telling what happened from that character's point of view.
Student will also draw a picture to go along with the journal entry.
At the end of the book, student will staple all the journal entries together to form a complete booklet.
They can even create a special cover for it from construction paper.

Vocabulary word: _____
Definition of the word: _____
_____
_____

Antonym of the word: _____
How many syllables does the word have? _____

Vocabulary Word: _____
Sentence using the word: _____
_____
_____

Synonym of the word: _____

**Vocabulary:** Student will use the vocabulary words from the list for this lesson. On one of the patterns, or on one index card they will write one vocabulary word. They should also write the definition of the word, then the Antonym and how many Syllables the word has.

On the other card, the student will write the same word. They will write a full sentence using this word and then write the Synonym of the word.

They will repeat this for all the vocabulary words in this lesson.

Place the patterns or cards in an envelope which can be glued into the student's notebook or onto the lapbook..

**Sequencing:** At the end of the lesson the student will write two of the main events on these two strips. Save them in an envelope which can be glued onto the lapbook or in the notebook. At the end of the book, these strips can be taken out and the student can arrange them in the correct order as they occurred in the story.

**Handwriting:** Student will pick their favorite sentence that they read in this lesson. Have them write the sentence in their best handwriting on this page or in their notebook.

**Student will write out the answers for the following:**
**Main Idea**: In a sentence or two, write what the main idea was of this section.
_____
_____
_____
_____
_____
_____

**Key Event:** In a sentence or two write what the most important event was in this section.
_____
_____
_____
_____
_____
_____

**Prediction:** In a sentence of two write what you Predict will happen in the next section.
_____
_____
_____
_____
_____
_____

**Comparison:** In a sentence of two compare two things in this section.  Tell what makes them alike and what makes them different.
_____
_____
_____
_____
_____
_____

**Fact or Opinion:** In one sentence write a fact about this section and one sentence that is an opinion about the lesson.
_____
_____
_____
_____
_____

**Descriptions:** Authors use descriptive words so that the reader can imagine the place or thing that is being described. Student will find one place in the book that the author really described well and write the name of the place inside the polygon. On the lines coming out of the polygon, student will write the words the author used to describe the place such as pretty, dark, blue....

**Poetry Form:** Student will write a poem about the book or characters using this format.

**Diamanté:** A diamanté is a seven-line, diamond-shaped poem which contrasts two opposites. The pattern is: First Line and seventh line - Name the opposites. Second and sixth lines - Two adjectives describing the opposite nearest it. Third and fifth lines - Three participles (ing words) describing the nearest opposite.
Fourth line - two nouns for each of the opposites.

Example:
   Fish
silvered, baited
teeming, swimming, darting
scaled amphibian, graceful hind
running, leaping, grazing
hunted, mammal
Deer

**Newspaper Activity:** Student will use this form to write their newspaper piece on then paste it onto their newspaper lay out poster.

**Sports Section:** Student will imagine that one of the characters in your book is in a sports competition and write a newspaper article about it and then illustrate it as well.

# Sports

**Creative Writing Activity:** **Memoir:** When writing a memoir, a person chooses one time or one event and expounds upon it by stretching the truth. Student will write a memoir as if they were a character in the story. They should choose one event to write about, and stretch the truth in the retelling.

My Memoir

**Writing Skills Activity:** Student will use this form or write in their notebook.

**Sequel:** A sequel is a movie or book that follows another. The sequel contains the same characters and follows the same story line. The characters and story line may change during the sequel but they have to start out the same to show the connection with the previous story. Students will write the first few paragraphs of a sequel for this story.

**Writing Skills Activity:** Student will use this form or write in their notebook.

**Lapbook Activity: Book Cover Puzzle:** Student will glue a picture they print from the internet of the book cover, onto this puzzle pattern so that the pattern shows on the back. Then student will cut the book cover into puzzle pieces. This can go in an envelope on the lapbook to be put together later.

## Poster Board Activity:
### Board Game
Student will create a board game on the poster board to use with this story.

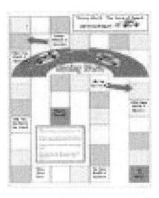

## Creative Art Activity:
### Photography
Photography is a great form of art. Student will find things that reminds them of this book and take some photos of it. Get these printed in black and white and some in color. Student can turn these into cards, frame them or take photos of one item in different angles and create a unique photo like this one.

# Lesson 9
# Activity

**Lesson 9 Activities:** Students will use the book they are studying and information found on the internet for the following activities. Then the student will write the information required for this activity on the patterns or in their notebook. The patterns may be cut out and placed on the lapbook.

**Encyclopedia:**
Student will choose one subject from this lesson that interested them and look it up on the internet or in encyclopedia. They will write the name of the subject across the top of the monitor pattern. On the monitor screen section, they will write three or more interesting facts about the subject.

**Journal:**
Student will imagine that they are one of the characters from the story. After reading each lesson, they will write a short journal entry telling what happened from that character's point of view.
Student will also draw a picture to go along with the journal entry.
At the end of the book, student will staple all the journal entries together to form a complete booklet.
They can even create a special cover for it from construction paper.

Vocabulary word: _____
Definition of the word: _____
_____
_____

Antonym of the word: _____
How many syllables does the word have? _____

Vocabulary Word: _____
Sentence using the word: _____
_____
_____

Synonym of the word: _____

_____
_____
_____
_____
_____
_____
_____

**Vocabulary:** Student will use the vocabulary words from the list for this lesson. On one of the patterns, or on one index card they will write one vocabulary word. They should also write the definition of the word, then the Antonym and how many Syllables the word has.

On the other card, the student will write the same word. They will write a full sentence using this word and then write the Synonym of the word.

They will repeat this for all the vocabulary words in this lesson.

Place the patterns or cards in an envelope which can be glued into the student's notebook or onto the lapbook..

**Sequencing:** At the end of the lesson the student will write two of the main events on these two strips. Save them in an envelope which can be glued onto the lapbook or in the notebook. At the end of the book, these strips can be taken out and the student can arrange them in the correct order as they occurred in the story.

**Handwriting:** Student will pick their favorite sentence that they read in this lesson. Have them write the sentence in their best handwriting on this page or in their notebook.

**Student will write out the answers for the following:**
**Main Idea**: In a sentence or two, write what the main idea was of this section.

**Key Event**: In a sentence or two write what the most important event was in this section.

**Prediction**: In a sentence of two write what you Predict will happen in the next section.

**Comparison**: In a sentence of two compare two things in this section. Tell what makes them alike and what makes them different.

**Fact or Opinion**: In one sentence write a fact about this section and one sentence that is an opinion about the lesson.

**Pyramid of Importance**: Each character in the story holds a position of importance. Some are of main importance, some are of less importance. Student will fill in the pyramid with the names of the characters. The top should have the most important character, the next line the next most important characters and continue down until you have listed all the characters in order of importance.

**Poetry Form:** Student will write a poem about the book or characters using this format.

**Lantern:** A lantern is a five line poem in the shape of a Japanese lantern. The Pattern is:

Line 1: noun (one syllable)
Line 2: describe the noun (two syllables)
Line 3: describe the noun (three syllables)
Line 4: describe the noun (four syllables)
Line 5: Synonym for noun in line one (one syllable)

| Example: | Mane |
|---|---|
| | long, thick |
| | blonde to black |
| | royal mantle |
| | Fur |

**Newspaper Activity:** Student will use this form to write their newspaper piece on then paste it onto their newspaper lay out poster.

**Entertainment Section: Book Review** Student will write an over all review of the book and tell what they liked and did not like, which characters seemed real and which scenes were described the best. Student should also ad a picture of the book cover.

# Book Review

**Creative Writing Activity: Newberry Award:** Each year one book is chosen to receive the John Newberry Award for great writing. Student will write a short report on why this book did or should have won the award.

**Writing Skills Activity:** Student will use this form or write in their notebook.

**Climax:** The climax of a story is the point where the reader knows who wins the conflict or how the problem will be solved. Student will write what the main problem was and at what point they knew how it would be solved.

**Lapbook Activity: Mini Book:** Student will make a mini book about this story or about a subject in the story. See the pattern on one of the following pages.

## Poster Board Activity:
**Door Sign**
Student will make a door sign from the pattern further on.

## Creative Art Activity:
**Parade Float**
Student will imagine that their town is hosting a parade to honor the author of this book and create a parade float from recycled boxes etc. to represent the over all book.

**Door Sign:** On a piece of poster board student will create a sign for their bedroom door that represents something from the book.

**Mini Book** : Student will create a mini book that retells the story. This may be put on the Lapbook.

12          1

*Print double sided. Cut on the red lines. Fold on the dotted lines.*

10 | 3

8 | 5

*Print double sided. Cut on the red lines. Fold on the dotted lines.*

| 4 | 9 |
| 6 | 7 |

# Lesson 10
# Activities

**Lesson 10 Activities:** Students will use the book they are studying and information found on the internet for the following activities. Then the student will write the information required for this activity on the patterns or in their notebook. The patterns may be cut out and placed on the lapbook.

**Encyclopedia:**
Student will choose one subject from this lesson that interested them and look it up on the internet or in encyclopedia. They will write the name of the subject across the top of the monitor pattern. On the monitor screen section, they will write three or more interesting facts about the subject.

**Journal:**
Student will imagine that they are one of the characters from the story. After reading each lesson, they will write a short journal entry telling what happened from that character's point of view.
Student will also draw a picture to go along with the journal entry.
At the end of the book, student will staple all the journal entries together to form a complete booklet.
They can even create a special cover for it from construction paper.

Vocabulary word: _____
Definition of the word: _____
_____
_____

Antonym of the word: _____
How many syllables does the word have? _____

Vocabulary Word: _____
Sentence using the word: _____
_____
_____

Synonym of the word: _____

**Vocabulary:** Student will use the vocabulary words from the list for this lesson. On one of the patterns, or on one index card they will write one vocabulary word. They should also write the definition of the word, then the Antonym and how many Syllables the word has.

On the other card, the student will write the same word. They will write a full sentence using this word and then write the Synonym of the word.

They will repeat this for all the vocabulary words in this lesson.

Place the patterns or cards in an envelope which can be glued into the student's notebook or onto the lapbook..

**Sequencing:** At the end of the lesson the student will write two of the main events on these two strips. Save them in an envelope which can be glued onto the lapbook or in the notebook. At the end of the book, these strips can be taken out and the student can arrange them in the correct order as they occurred in the story.

**Handwriting:** Student will pick their favorite sentence that they read in this lesson. Have them write the sentence in their best handwriting on this page or in their notebook.

**Student will write out the answers for the following:**

**Main Idea**: In a sentence or two, write what the main idea was of this section.

_____
_____
_____
_____
_____
_____

**Key Event:** In a sentence or two write what the most important event was in this section.

_____
_____
_____
_____
_____
_____

**Prediction:** In a sentence of two write what you Predict will happen in the next section.

_____
_____
_____
_____
_____
_____

**Comparison:** In a sentence of two compare two things in this section. Tell what makes them alike and what makes them different.

_____
_____
_____
_____
_____
_____

**Fact or Opinion:** In one sentence write a fact about this section and one sentence that is an opinion about the lesson.

_____
_____
_____
_____
_____

**Hero vs. Villain:** Most stories usually have a hero (the main character) and a villain. The villain may not seem that bad. The villain is usually the character who stands in the way of the main character, or against the main character. Student will name the Hero and the Villain and fill in the "What the Villain does...." square.

## What the Villain does to hinder the Hero.

## Hero

## Villain

**Poetry Form:** Student will write a poem about the book or characters using this format.

**Shape Poem:** To be done on a separate sheet of paper. Shape poems can be made by placing words, which describe a particular object, in such a way that they form the shape of the object. Student will start by making a simple outline of the shape or object (an animal, a football, a fruit etc.) large enough to fill a piece of paper. Then student will brainstorm a minimum of ten words and phrases that describe the shape including action and feeling words as well. Next, student will place a piece of paper over the shape and decide where the words are going to be placed so that they outline the shape but also fit well together. Separate words and phrases with commas. Shape poems can also be created by simply filling in the shape with a poem, as well.

**Newspaper Activity:** Student will use this form to write their newspaper piece on then paste it onto their newspaper lay out poster.

**Word Search Section:   Find all the words**

```
C O M B I N A T I O N Y T N U O C I D D
R S U S M T R D G A L L O N S L A N E P
Y T S U I N I F E E F S J W E U D T T O
S R H O S A O L T G S R E V T G E E A S
T A R R E T V A T E A D E O D R T R D T
A N O E R R R B L H C R M E M A C E I P
L G O G A O E B X W E A U I Z V E S P O
S E M N B P S E O S T R N O B E P T A N
M L S A L M E R T I J E M N C L X I L I
A Y L D E I R G C E D Z Q O E S E N I N
R E S N O I T A N I C C A V M D I G D G
T A I T S R L S A S S E M B L E D D R N
I D L O E L G T O E D I S G U S T E D I
F O M U Y R F E R O T A R O P A V E E Y
I E B O C Z I D H O N E Y C O M B S R F
C H E R M I T O Y L G N I S U C C A O I
I S T S U R T S U O I C I P S U S D N N
A B L I Z Z A R D S T A N C H I O N S G
L Q F A M I L I A R E P U T A T I O N A
S E R U S A E R T P E G E L I V I R P M
```

| | | | |
|---|---|---|---|
| ACCUSINGLY | ARTIFICIAL | HERMIT | HONEYCOMBS |
| ASSEMBLED | AUTOMATICALLY | IMPORTANT | INTERESTING |
| BLIZZARD | CANNED | LESSON | MAGNIFYING |
| CLEVEREST | COMBINATION | MISERABLE | MUSHROOMS |
| COUNTY | CRYSTALS | MYSTERIOUS | PARTICULAR |
| DANGEROUS | DETERMINED | POSTPONING | PRIVILEGE |
| DEW | DILAPIDATED | REPUTATION | RESERVOIR |
| DISCOURAGED | DISGUSTED | SNORE | STANCHIONS |
| ELABORATELY | EVAPORATOR | STRANGELY | SUSPICIOUS |
| EXPECTED | FAMILIAR | THERMOMETER | TREASURES |
| FLABBERGASTED | FREEZE | TRUSTS | VACCINATIONS |
| GALLONS | GRAVEL | WORRISOME | |

**Creative Writing Activity: A Different End:** Student will write a different ending for the story.

# Writing Skills Activity: Plot Analysis Board
Student will create this by following the directions.

What you need:
Index Cards, Pictures from the internet, Markers, Crayons. Glue

1. Fold the poster board in half so that it makes a folder.
2. Decorate the front of the folder with pictures and information that includes the Title, the Author, the Illustrator, and the Publisher.
3. On index cards, write the information requested below. Glue the index cards inside the folder. You can put pictures on the cards to go along with them.
   Information to put on cards:
   1. Main Character and Character Traits
   2. Main Setting
   3. Other Characters
   4. Other Settings in the Story
   5. Main Problem
   6. Other Problems
   7. Climax
   8. Solution to the Problem
   9. Your favorite part of the story
   10. What you would change if you could about the story.

**Lapbook Activity: The Commandments:** Student will cut out the patter and fold so that the Ten Commandments are on the front. Inside student will write how a character may have broken or upheld one or more of these commandments. Attach to Lapbook.

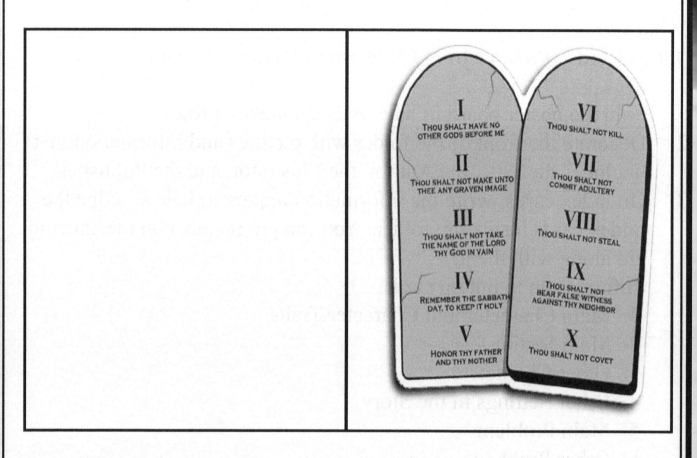

## Poster Board Activity:
### Jeopardy
On the poster board student will create a game board like the one on the next page. They will cut out several sets of the play money. The teacher will write 4 to 8 questions for each category. The student then picks one category and the dollar amount of the question they will try and answer. The teacher or student reads the question. If the answer is correct the student wins the amount of money that they chose. The next player takes a turn. The winner is the one with the most

## Creative Art Activity:
### Sketch
Student will imagine they are a sketch artist and using black pencils or charcoal pencils, they will sketch some of the main characters, places or events from the story.

# JEOPARDY

| People | Places | Animals | Other |
|--------|--------|---------|-------|
| $100 | $100 | $100 | $100 |
| $200 | $200 | $200 | $200 |
| $300 | $300 | $300 | $300 |
| $400 | $400 | $400 | $400 |

# Additional Activities

# Additional Writing Activities

Imaginative: Imaginative writing is when you write a fanciful story using your imagination. Student will write one that comes to mind while they read this book.

Essay: An essay is a short piece of writing, from an author's personal point of view. Student will write a short essay from their point of view about a subject that comes to mind while reading these books.

Speech: A speech is the act of delivering a formal spoken communication to an audience . Student will write a short speech that one of the characters from the books may have given.

Autobiography: An autobiography is a story of a person's life. Student will write a short autobiography outline of one of the characters or they could write about the author as well.

Humor: Humor allows the reader to laugh and enjoy a story. Student will write a humorous piece about a subject or thing mentioned in these books.

ABC Story: ABC Stories are short stories that have each sentence starting with the next letter in the alphabet. Student will write a short ABC story about an event or one of the characters in the book. For example:
A girl named Kit lived in America. By noon she was happy...

**Literature Web:** A story will make you think of many things and feel many things. Student will draw this chart in their notebook and fill it in.

Key Words: What were some important words or phrases?

Feelings: What feelings did you have while reading the book?

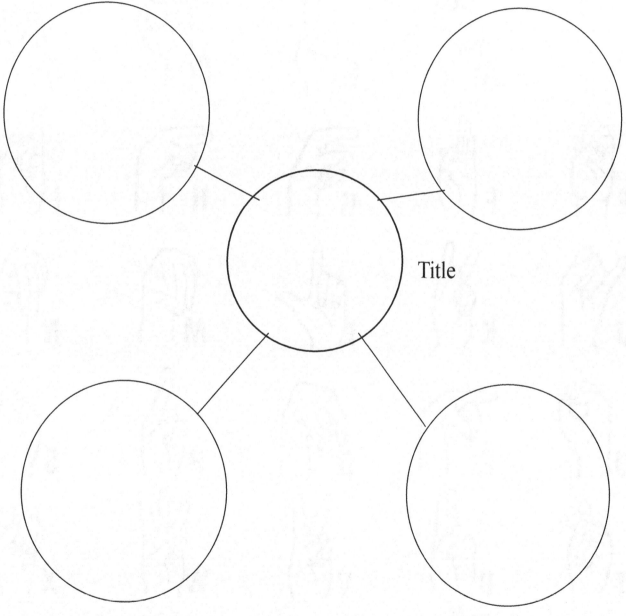

Symbols: Did the author use any symbols in the story?

Attitude: What do you think the authors attitude is about the subject this story is about?

**Sign Language:**
On a piece of poster board, student will glue a larger versions of the sign language alphabet. Now the teacher will sign a name, scene or vocabulary word from the story. Students try to figure the word out by pointing to the correct sign language letter and spelling out the words.

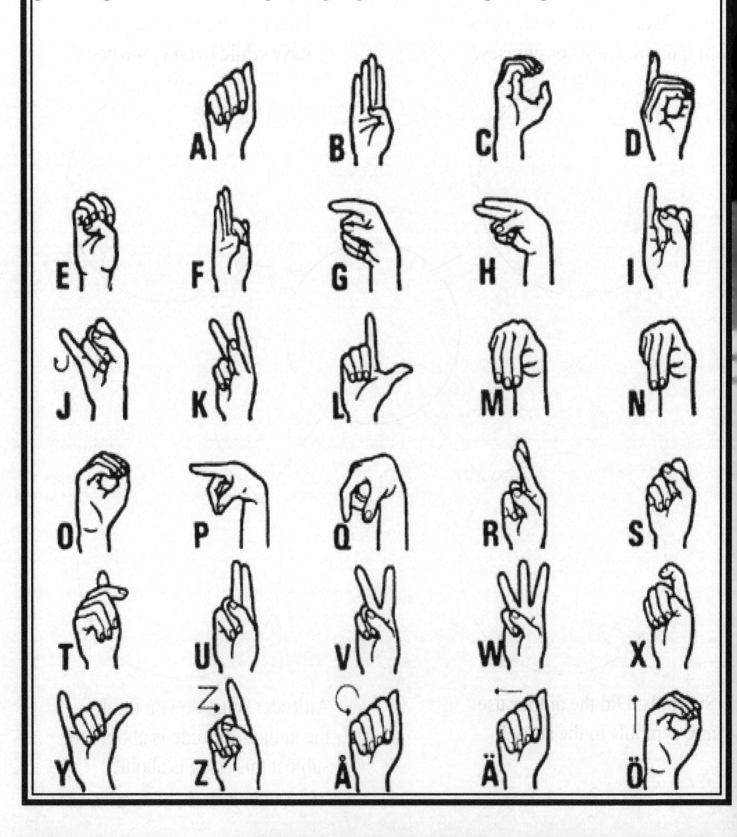

**Theater Box:**

Get a cardboard box with a flat side larger than a piece of paper. In the side cut out a square about 6 by 9 inches. This will be the opening for your theater.

While reading each chapter of the book, Student will draw one or more of the main scenes on 8 1/2 by 11 inch drawing paper. Stay within the inner 6 by 9 inches though. Color these with markers, paint, colored pencils etc.

Figure out a way that these pictures can be slid in and out of the box, so they appear in the opening and it looks like you are changing scenes, or draw them all on one long roll, and create rollers in each end of the box out of paper towel rolls.

At the end of the book you should have a whole story in these scenes. Present the scenes in your theater to family or friends. You will have to act as the announcer and explain the main events in each scene.

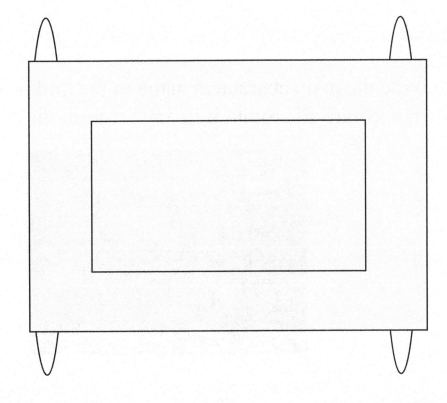

## Acting: Student will

1. Dress up as one of the characters in the story. They can act out their favorite part of the story.
2. Host a talk show where another member of the family acts as the television host. Your student is the main character of the story. They ask you questions about the story.
3. Hold a trial. Someone dresses up as the villain in the story. Someone dresses up as the main character. Someone as a lawyer and someone as a judge. Hold a trial to determine if the villain is really guilty of crimes or not.

## Rock Art:
Student will gather smooth rocks of different shapes and sizes. Student will clean the rocks and when dry create characters from the book with the rocks, by painting them, making clothes for them and gluing on google eyes.

## Name Art:
Student will write the main characters name in the middle of 1/4 poster board and then decorate all around it in any art form they like.

## Carving:

Use soap or wax and carve a character from the story. All you need to carve soap is a bar of soap and a spoon. If your child is old enough to use a butter knife then you can let them have a butter knife to carve their soap with. Soap carving can be messy so it is best to be done on a table covered with an old cloth or newspaper. And everyone doing the carving should have old clothes on.

When carving soap, you can use any size bar of soap you would like, but a nice big bar of soap is better to get creative with. If you are lucky enough to have a bar of home made lye soap that will work as well. Unwrap your bar of soap and decide what you want to make with your bar of soap. Soap is a soft material so a spoon will work to carve a bar of soap just fine. A knife can give your bar of soap more detail then a spoon can but it is more dangerous.

## Sewing:

Use felt and material stuffing. Create a pattern for something from the story such as an animal or character. Cut out two of the same patterns from the felt. Have student sew around the outside edges. Stuff with stuffing and complete the sewing.

## Design a Needlepoint:
Get graph paper and have student design a needlepoint by placing an x in the boxes to design the picture.

**Shape Puzzle**: On poster board student will draw out a large copy of the shape of a character or item from the book. Cut it into a puzzle pattern.

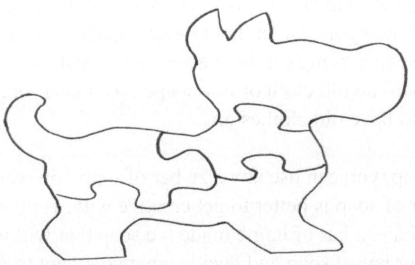

**I Spy**

Student will find pictures on the internet of things that come to mind while reading this book. Pictures of the characters, of the vocabulary words etc. Student will print and then glue them all over the poster board. Now they should make an I spy set of calling cards on index cards.
For example your cards would say:
I spy a cat.
I spy a rat.
Give the cards to a younger child and see if they can find all the items on the I spy poster.

**Bingo:** Print as many of these Bingo boards as you need for the students. Write the vocabulary words in the squares of the Bingo boards. Each board should be different. Use the definition index cards as the call cards for the game.

| B | I | N | G | O |
|---|---|---|---|---|
|   |   |   |   |   |
|   |   |   |   |   |
|   |   | Free Space |   |   |
|   |   |   |   |   |
|   |   |   |   |   |

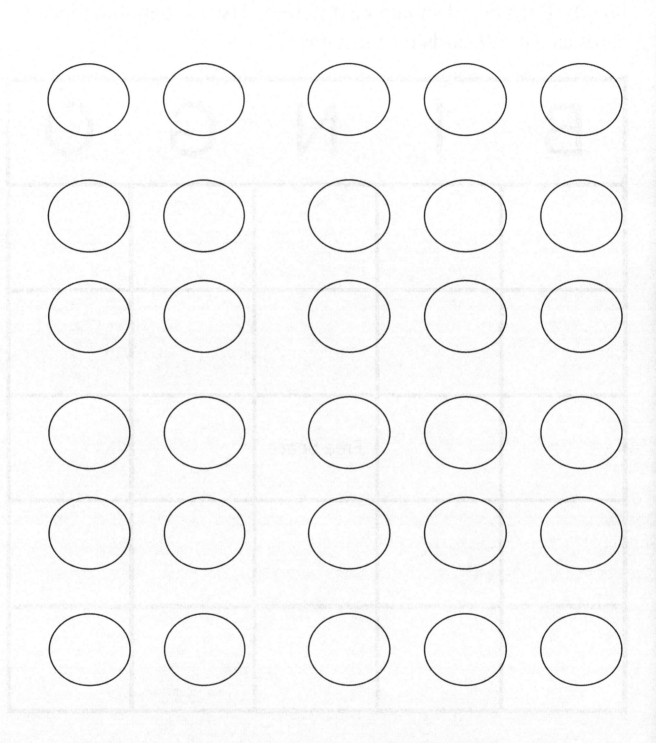

# Comprehension

The following pages have the
Fill in the Blanks,
True and False,
Multiple Choice
and
Who, What, Where, When,
Why and How Questions
for all lessons.

Use the Vocabulary words
on the following page for the
questions

| Lesson 1  | Chapter | 1,2   |
|-----------|---------|-------|
| Lesson 2  | Chapter | 3,4   |
| Lesson 3  | Chapter | 5     |
| Lesson 4  | Chapter | 6     |
| Lesson 5  | Chapter | 7     |
| Lesson 6  | Chapter | 8     |
| Lesson 7  | Chapter | 9     |
| Lesson 8  | Chapter | 10    |
| Lesson 9  | Chapter | 11,12 |
| Lesson 10 | Chapter | 13,14 |

**Vocabulary Words:**

Lesson 1. worrisome privilege penned discouraged nuisance flabbergasted disgusted expected determined dilapidated

Lesson 2. treasures automatically reservoir elaborately musty combination evaporator gallons science thermometer

Lesson 3. miracle blizzard billowing almanac gravel interesting crystals kindling frosty jealous

Lesson 4. explorer steel ordinary journal particular brambles lichens marigold swamp swelled

Lesson 5. slippery hummocks magnifying meanders mushrooms immense cleverest bounty snore

Lesson 6. promoted restful dew trusts possible entirely hermit honeycombs totem gourd

Lesson 7. ripened canned mysterious important postponing accusingly miserable stanchions telescope different

Lesson 8. scarlet county dangerous gymnasium skeletons month artificial entitled weather possessed

Lesson 9. worst assembled syrup cicadas strain filter numbness impatient expected freeze

Lesson 10. familiar vaccinations truant specimens hooky suspicious converted appetite strangely reputation

Lesson 1

Fill in the Blanks: Write the vocabulary word that best completes the sentence.
Words:           determined    expected    disgusted    penned

1. Grandma thought that the children were too used to being _____ up in the big city.
2. Marley knew that her dad would be _____ with her bragging.
3. Dinner was on the table in a few minutes because Mrs. Chris had _____ her guests to arrive at any moment.
4. Joe was _____ to be the first one to see Maple Hill.

True / False: Write T if statement is true; write F if it is false.

1. _____ Marley's father had been a soldier and a prisoner of war.
2. _____ The only place worth anything is where a child can go out and run as he pleases.
3. _____ People told Marley's mother not to worry about Daddy when he was missing because he would be back.
4. _____ Grandma's place is still well kept and looks like new.

Multiple Choice: Write ABCD in the space for the best answer.

1. _____ Where is Maple Hill?
A. New York
B. Pennsylvania
C. California
D. Florida

2. _____ What does Marley's father need to get better?
A. a week at the beach
B. a movie
C. the fresh outdoors
D. a good doctor

3. _____ What did Marley's great-grandmother say was the first miracle?
A. when the sap came up
B. when the apple blossoms open
C. when the first snow comes
D. when the corn grows

4. _____ Mr. and Mrs. Chris were _____ of Marley's mother when she was a little girl.
A. relatives
B. tour guides
C. park rangers
D. good neighbors

Lesson 1

Write full sentences for this section:

1. Who hated cities?
2. What did mother feel about Maple Hill?
3. Where did Mrs. Chris see Dale before?
4. When mother used to visit Maple Hill what time of the year was it?
5. Why are buckets hanging in the maple trees?
6. How did Dale get in the newspaper?

(Who) _____
_____
_____
_____

(What) _____
_____
_____
_____

(Where) _____
_____
_____
_____

(When) _____
_____
_____
_____

(Why) _____
_____
_____
_____

(How) _____
_____
_____
_____

Lesson 2

Fill in the Blanks: Write the vocabulary word that best completes the sentence.

Words:   combination   musty   treasures   evaporator

1. The dusty and musty old house was full of _____ and surprises.
2. The pillows smelled _____ so Marley's mother hung them out under the sun and fresh air.
3. The _____ of cold and freezing nights, plus warm days helps to bring the tree sap up.
4. The _____ boils the water out of the sap and leaves the sweet syrup behind.

True / False: Write T if statement is true; write F if it is false.

1. _____ Rainwater is so soft it makes soap foamy and full of suds.
2. _____ People can pump oil, water, and sap from the ground.
3. _____ An average maple tree can give twenty gallons of sap in a season which can produce a half gallon of syrup.
4. _____ A maple tree thats two hundred years old is still young for a tree.

Multiple Choice: Write ABCD in the space for the best answer.

1. _____ What kind of water comes from rainwater?
A. soft water
B. mud water
C. blue water
D. hard water

2. _____ What was everywhere in the old house?
A. ripped carpets
B. broken windows
C. mouse droppings (leavings)
D. leaky pipes

3. _____ What treasure did Joe and Dad find in the barn?
A. an old buggy
B. a sleigh
C. a plow
D. both A and B

4. _____ How many meadow mice babies can one mother mouse make in a year?
A. 10
B. 1,000
C. 200
D. 50

Lesson 2
Write full sentences for this section:

1. Who owns an old maple tree that can give over two hundred forty gallons a season?
2. What did Mr. Chris use to stop the bubbles from boiling over?
3. Where is Mr. Chris's sugar camp?
4. When Mr. Chris's two hundred year old tree dies what is he going to do with it?
5. Why is spring a miracle?
6. How did Marley's father feel as he explored the old house?

(Who) _____
_____
_____
_____

(What) _____
_____
_____
_____

(Where) _____
_____
_____
_____

(When) _____
_____
_____
_____

(Why) _____
_____
_____
_____

(How) _____
_____
_____
_____

Lesson 3

Fill in the Blanks: Write the vocabulary word that best completes the sentence.
Words:                gravel    blizzard    crystals    miracle

1. Mr. Chris kept his promises because once spring came one _____ at a time was nothing.
2. When the family was returning to Maple Hill a huge _____ left a foot of snow on the road.
3. Maple Hill now had _____ on the road making driving much easier.
4. The sun came up and it was clear and frosty leaving a million _____ shining on the trees.

True / False: Write T if statement is true; write F if it is false.

1. _____ It was almost April now and Mr. Chris was still working in the sugar house.
2. _____ A Franklin stove is an open fireplace with a screen in front of it.
3. _____ Marley burned the farmhouse down.
4. _____ Marley's dad taught her how to use the stove.

Multiple Choice: Write ABCD in the space for the best answer.

1. _____ Mr. Chris says that nothing is as important in the country as the _____.
A. lakes
B. streams
C. weather
D. moon

2. _____ What did Mr. Chris give Dad?
A. Field and Stream Magazine
B. The Almanac
C. Farmers Guide
D. Organic Farming Magazine

3. _____ Daddy said that skunk cabbage is _____.
A. interesting
B. ugly
C. beautiful
D. all the above

4. _____ How many pancakes did Joe eat?
A. 9
B. 3
C. 4
D. 6

Lesson 3

Write full sentences for this section:

1. Who snuck out early in the morning before anyone else was up?
2. What is Dad and Marley going to do for mother?
3. Where did Dale eat while the family was in the city?
4. When mother saw the fire what was the first thing that went to her head?
5. Why was Marley's dad going to be madder than she had ever seen him before?
6. How did Marley's dad put out the fire in the stove?

(Who) _____
_____
_____

(What) _____
_____
_____

(Where) _____
_____
_____

(When) _____
_____
_____

(Why) _____
_____
_____

(How) _____
_____
_____

Lesson 4

Fill in the Blanks: Write the vocabulary word that best completes the sentence.
Words:           ordinary    swamp    journal    explorer

1. When other boys wanted to be a policeman or cowboys, Joe was going to be an _____.
2. Mr. Chris knows all the common _____ everyday names of all the folks in Maple Hill.
3. Grandma wrote in her _____ everyday about all the new things she learned and saw.
4. The cows were pounding up the very _____ that Marley was stuck in.

True / False: Write T if statement is true; write F if it is false.

1. _____ Joe liked to explore new places with his friends tagging along behind him.
2. _____ If someone eats a bloodroot their heart will stop in a day.
3. _____ Mr. Chris made Marley feel like every flower was a special old friend.
4. _____ When Marley looked up she saw a huge buffalo running towards her.

Multiple Choice: Write ABCD in the space for the best answer.

1. _____ What is the big affair going on in the woods?
A. a carnival
B. a circus
C. a flower beauty contest
D. a state fair

2. _____ Why do people call hepatica a good medicine for the liver?
A. the leaves are the shape of a liver
B. the color of the flower is the same as a liver
C. the shape of the flower is like a liver
D. the color of the leaves are like a liver

3. _____ What are some other words for the hepatica flower?
A. liverwort
B. herb trinity
C. squirrel cup and mouse ear
D. all the above

4. _____ Violets come in what colors?
A. white and yellow
B. blue and purple
C. striped and spotted
D. all the above

Lesson 4

Write full sentences for this section:

1. Who used to keep a journal about her garden and the flowers in the woods and fields?
2. What did Marley bring mother everyday?
3. Where did Marley's really scary adventure take place?
4. When did Marley's really scary adventure take place?
5. Why can't Marley pretend like Joe does?
6. How did Marley slow up Joe on his exploring trips?

(Who) _____
_____
_____
_____

(What) _____
_____
_____
_____

(Where) _____
_____
_____
_____

(When) _____
_____
_____
_____

(Why) _____
_____
_____
_____

(How) _____
_____
_____
_____

Lesson 5

Fill in the Blanks: Write the vocabulary word that best completes the sentence.
Words:          mushrooms    slippery    immense    magnifying

1. Mother called the drive up to Maple Hill the great _____.
2. Joe brought along his _____ glass so he could gaze into the strangest worlds.
3. During the autumn _____ grow throughout the woods.
4. The _____ limbs of the old maple tree crashed to the ground.

True / False: Write T if statement is true; write F if it is false.

1. _____ Joe was not finished with his exploring so he wouldn't let Marley tag along.
2. _____ At one time the ocean was practically everywhere.
3. _____ Foxes have been raiding Mr. Chris's hen house.
4. _____ A male fox feeds his family and will lead enemies away from the den.

Multiple Choice: Write ABCD in the space for the best answer.

1. _____ What did Joe find in the stream bed?
A. ancient see shells
B. a crab
C. tiny shrimp
D. a lot of cans

2. _____ What is the name of the toadstool that lights up at night?
A. Sunflower Cups
B. Jack-o O-Lantern
C. Yellow Buttercups
D. Yellow Bells

3. _____ How many foxes were there?
A. three
B. two
C. five
D. seven

4. _____ How did Joe get the fox family to leave?
A. he beat on drums
B. he laid a trail of meat far away from the den
C. he put a burning rag in the back door of the den
D. he yelled as loud as he could

Lesson 5
Write full sentences for this section:

1. Who told Joe about everything on Maple Hill?
2. What happened to the chestnut trees on Maple Hill?
3. Where did Joe take Marley to explore?
4. When Joe and Fritz found the fox den what did they find?
5. Why did Joe walk in a certain easy way?
6. How did Mr. Chris know the age of the old maple tree?

(Who) _____
_____
_____
_____

(What) _____
_____
_____
_____

(Where ) _____
_____
_____
_____

(When) _____
_____
_____
_____

(Why) _____
_____
_____
_____

(How) _____
_____
_____
_____

Lesson 6

Fill in the Blanks: Write the vocabulary word that best completes the sentence.
Words:         honeycombs    restful    possible    hermit

1. Marley could hear the _____ sound of water splashing down the hill.
2. Dale believed that it was still _____ for a family to live off of the land.
3. Joe was up and ready to see the _____ Mr. Chris told him about.
4. In the hermit's mailbox there were a pile of _____ and a note.

True / False: Write T if statement is true; write F if it is false.

1. _____ Dad hated gardening so the family will have to go to town to get groceries.
2. _____ Mother had found surprise after surprise in Grandma's old garden.
3. _____ Joe was shocked to see Marley had followed him.
4. _____ Looking into the hermit's spring house was like looking at long ago.


Multiple Choice: Write ABCD in the space for the best answer.

1. _____ What did Dale make for dinner?
A. fried Chicken and corn on the cob
B. chicken soup and dumplings
C. broiled steak
D. a turkey dinner with all the trimmings

2. _____ When is the family returning to the city?
A. the end of summer
B. not until the leaves turn
C. just before winter
D. both A and B

3. _____ What are the little red points sticking up our of the ground?
A. rhubarb
B. iris
C. snapdragons
D. beets

4. _____ What is written on the note in the hermit's mailbox?
A. take honey
B. leave money
C. gone for the day
D. all the above

Lesson 6

Write full sentences for this section:

1. Who was a born fisherman?
2. What does the old hermit like to make?
3. Where does Harry the hermit live?
4. When there was a knock at the door after supper who was it?
5. Why is Marley glade she wasn't a boy?
6. How does the hermit keep his food cold?

(Who) _____
_____
_____
_____

(What) _____
_____
_____
_____

(Where) _____
_____
_____
_____

(When) _____
_____
_____
_____

(Why) _____
_____
_____
_____

(How) _____
_____
_____
_____

Lesson 7

Fill in the Blanks: Write the vocabulary word that best completes the sentence.
Words:          telescope     ripened     important     canned

1. The summer world on Maple Hill grew, blossomed, and _____.
2. Mom _____ all the vegetables and fruits that Dad had grown over the summer.
3. When Marley came down the stairs she heard Dale say something mysterious and _____.
4. Harry took Marley to the meadow to look through his _____.

True / False: Write T if statement is true; write F if it is false.

1. _____ On the Fourth of July it was so hot the ice cream melted before anyone could eat it.
2. _____ Pokeberry juice was the most delicious juice Marley had ever tasted.
3. _____ The school in Maple Hill is small and teaches the older kids along with the younger.
4. _____ Harry believed that everyone on a farm should care for something alive and useful.

Multiple Choice: Write ABCD in the space for the best answer.

1. _____ Summer time is what time for fruit trees?
A. a time to prune
B. a time to harvest
C. a time to graft
D. a time to fertilize

2. _____ What do people make with all kinds of berries?
A. jelly
B. pies
C. preserves
D. all the above

3. _____ What did Mr. Chris make with pokeberries?
A. jelly
B. juice
C. ink
D. preserves

4. _____ In Mexico what do the Indians use to make their fences?
A. cactus
B. wood
C. chain link
D. vines

Lesson 7
Write full sentences for this section:

1. Who gave the children two goats and some chickens to take care of during the winter?
2. What important decision did the family make?
3. Where did Harry find names for his goats?
4. When the flowers bloom what happens?
5. Why did the family decide to stay in Maple Hill?
6. How could the goats help the family live in Maple Hill?

(Who) _____
_____
_____

(What) _____
_____
_____
_____

(Where) _____
_____
_____
_____

(When) _____
_____
_____
_____

(Why) _____
_____
_____
_____

(How) _____
_____
_____
_____

Lesson 8

Fill in the Blanks: Write the vocabulary word that best completes the sentence.
Words:         dangerous    scarlet    gymnasium    county

1. It was a beautiful world that Marley had awaken to, it was a _____ and golden miracle.
2. At the _____ Fair everyone puts their finest products on display to sell.
3. At the fair the indoor garden display is held in the school's _____.
4. Mushrooms are _____ unless you know which ones to pick.

True / False: Write T if statement is true; write F if it is false.

1. _____ At Joe's school the band leader assigned Joe to learn the drums.
2. _____ Mrs. Chris's chrysanthemums are as big as dinner plates.
3. _____ The mushroom called the Destroying Angel can kill a person in a few days.
4. _____ The freeze didn't hurt Mom and Dad's gardens.

Multiple Choice: Write ABCD in the space for the best answer.

1. _____ In Marley's little schoolhouse what was her first assignment?
A. read a book
B. draw maple leaves
C. copy the alphabet
D. recite a poem

2. _____ How often does the bookmobile visit the school?
A. once a month
B. once a week
C. every two months
D. every six weeks

3. _____ How did Maple Hill turn into different places?
A. it was brown then green
B. yellow and gold
C. white allover
D. all the above

4. _____ Where did Joe go?
A. to a school party
B. to a church party
C. to Harry's
D. to town for hot cocoa with a friend

Lesson 8
Write full sentences for this section:

1. Who had the best job at the fair?
2. What happened to Harry?
3. Where was the County Fair held?
4. When Christmas came how many Christmas trees did Marley have?
5. Why does Maple Mountain look like it's on fire?
6. How much did Miss Perkinsen have to know in her little schoolhouse?

(Who) _____
_____
_____
_____

(What) _____
_____
_____
_____

(Where ) _____
_____
_____
_____

(When) _____
_____
_____
_____

(Why) _____
_____
_____
_____

(How) _____
_____
_____
_____

Lesson 9

Fill in the Blanks: Write the vocabulary word that best completes the sentence.
Words:           assembled    worst    impatient    strain

1. A very heavy snow came and Mr. Chris said it was one of the _____ storms in history.
2. The evaporator is being _____ and will be ready for the upcoming sugaring.
3. The farmers have to _____ and filter the sap before it is usable.
4. Mother's voice sounded _____ but it was because she was worried.

True / False: Write T if statement is true; write F if it is false.

1. _____ Every hole and dipper had to be drilled in a new place on the tree.
2. _____ The holes in the trees are very harmful to the tree and they dry up after a few years.
3. _____ In the old days folks used to help each other more than they do now.
4. _____ Chrissie will not leave Mr. Chris until there is no more danger to his health.

Multiple Choice: Write ABCD in the space for the best answer.

1. _____ A week after Valentine's day what miracle happened?
A. it's sugaring time again
B. the saps up
C. the birds are returning
D. both A and B

2. _____ A _____ can tell a farmer what kind of a day the next day will be.
A. red sunset
B. black clouds
C. fog
D. white clouds

3. _____ How many buckets did they hang for Mr. Chris?
A. six hundred
B. three hundred fifty
C. over fourteen hundred
D. seven hundred and fifty

4. _____ What was the best thing anyone could do to help Mr. Chris?
A. cry
B. work
C. worry
D. give up

Lesson 9

Write full sentences for this section:

1. Who taught Mr. Chris's grandfather how to make maple syrup?
2. What happened to Mr. Chris?
3. Where was the best sugar year in history?
4. When Dale returned home how did he feel?
5. Why does Mr. Chris love sugaring time?
6. How warm does the air temperature have to be to bring up the sap?

(Who) _____

_____

_____

_____

(What) _____

_____

_____

_____

(Where) _____

_____

_____

_____

(When) _____

_____

_____

_____

(Why) _____

_____

_____

_____

(How) _____

_____

_____

_____

Lesson 10

Fill in the Blanks: Write the vocabulary word that best completes the sentence.
Words:          suspicious     appetite     truant     familiar

1. The visitor coming up the hill looked very _____ to Joe.
2. Miss Annie Nelson is the county _____ officer.
3. When Dale handed Miss Annie a cup of maple syrup, for a moment she was a little _____.
4. Mr. Chris had a really good _____ by the time he got home.

True / False: Write T if statement is true; write F if it is false.

1. _____ The kids at school call Miss Annie, Annie-Get-Your-Gun.
2. _____ When Miss Annie asked who discovered how to make maple syrup everyone said it was the Indians.
3. _____ The boys at school are going to take turns so they will not lose a lot of school time.
4. _____ Both the boys and girls from school are going to help out at the sugar camp.

Multiple Choice: Write ABCD in the space for the best answer.

1. _____ Who was the visitor?
A. the school nurse
B. the truant officer
C. the sheriff's deputy
D. both A and B

2. _____ What is Joe and Marley receiving for helping Mr. Chris?
A. free maple syrup
B. part of their education
C. wages
D. school merits

3. _____ What miracle did Miss Annie arrange?
A. ask the senior citizens to help at the camp
B. ask the town fire department to stop the sap from flowing
C. allow the boys from Joe's class to help Daddy and Fritz
D. Joe can stay home for the winter

4. _____ To welcome Mr. Chris home what gifts did Marley and Mother have ready for him?
A. a huge welcome back cake
B. a spring flower in a pot
C. homemade ice cream
D. both A and B

Lesson 10
Write full sentences for this section:

1. Who taught school before she married?
2. What did Miss Annie say was a part of our American heritage?
3. Where did Miss Annie live all her life?
4. When Miss Annie saw the sugar camp what did she do?
5. Why was Mr. Chris so excited with Marley's gift
6. How are the boys from school going to get to the sugar camp?

(Who) _____
_____
_____
_____

(What) _____
_____
_____
_____

(Where) _____
_____
_____
_____

(When) _____
_____
_____
_____

(Why) _____
_____
_____
_____

(How) _____
_____
_____
_____

Answer Key

Lesson 1

Fill in the Blanks
1. penned
2. disgusted
3. expected
4. determined

True and False
1. T
2. T
3. F
4. F

Multiple Choice
1. B
2. C
3. A
4. D

Who, What, Where, When, Why, and How
1. Marley's great grandmother
2. it was a place where miracles happen
3. in the newspaper
4. summer
5. they are collecting the sweet maple sap
6. he was a war hero

Lesson 2

Fill in the Blanks
1. treasures
2. musty
3. combination
4. evaporator

True and False
1. T
2. F
3. T
4. T

Multiple Choice
1. A
2. C
3. D
4. B

Who, What, Where, When, Why, and How
1. Mr. Chris
2. cream
3. in his sugar-house
4. it will provide logs for another season of sugaring
5. the trees come alive again
6. happy, cheerful, and interested

Lesson 3
Fill in the Blanks
1. miracle
2. blizzard
3. gravel
4. crystals
True and False
1. F
2. F
3. F
4. T
Multiple Choice
1. C
2. B
3. D
4. A
Who, What, Where, When, Why, and How
1. Joe
2. make breakfast
3. Chrissie's house
4. they didn't have a phone yet
5. Marley almost burned down the house
6. he pushed the damper on the stove

Lesson 4
Fill in the Blanks
1. explorer
2. ordinary
3. journal
4. swamp
True and False
1. F
2. T
3. T
4. F
Multiple Choice
1. C
2. A
3. D
4. D
Who, What, Where, When, Why, and How
1. Grandma
2. a bouquet of wild flowers
3. beyond the old pasture near the woods and into Mr. Chris's pasture
4. Easter vacation
5. she is always getting scared
6. she always wanted to stop and look at everything

Lesson 5
Fill in the Blanks
1. slippery
2. magnifying
3. mushrooms
4. immense
True and False
1. F
2. T
3. T
4. T
Multiple Choice
1. A
2. B
3. D
4. C
Who, What, Where, When, Why, and How
1. Mr. Chris
2. they got a disease and died
3. Maple Mountain
4. the foxes were gone and the den was full of stuff
5. he had learned Indian walk
6. he counts the rings in the center of the tree

Lesson 6
Fill in the Blanks
1. restful
2. possible
3. hermit
4. honeycombs
True and False
1. F
2. T
3. F
4. T
Multiple Choice
1. C
2. D
3. A
4. D
Who, What, Where, When, Why, and How
1. Joe
2. wooden chains
3. at the end of the mountain, south, just above the pond where the ducks land
4. the old hermit came to introduce himself and bring a gift to the family
5. it's alright for girls to be scared or silly or ask dumb questions
6. he had a spring house

Lesson 7
Fill in the Blanks
1. ripened
2. canned
3. important
4. telescope
True and False
1. T
2. F
3. F
4. T
Multiple Choice
1. B
2. D
3. C
4. A
Who, What, Where, When, Why, and How
1. Harry
2. to stay in Maple Hill for the rest of the year
3. Shakespeare
4. every flower bears some kind of seed or fruit
5. Daddy is better and they could live cheaper there
6. they give milk, butter, and cheese
Lesson 8
Fill in the Blanks
1. scarlet
2. county
3. gymnasium
4. dangerous
True and False
1. F
2. T
3. T
4. F
Multiple Choice
1. B
2. A
3. D
4. C
Who, What, Where, When, Why, and How
1. the judges
2. he slipped in the ice and hurt his leg and would have frozen if Joe hadn't come along
3. at Joe's school
4. three
5. the trees were red and yellow
6. she has to know everything about the six graders

Lesson 9
Fill in the Blanks
1. worst
2. assembled
3. strain
4. impatient
True and False
1. T
2. F
3. T
4. T
Multiple Choice
1. D
2. A
3. C
4. B
Who, What, Where, When, Why, and How
1. the Indians
2. he was numb and couldn't stand, he went to the hospital
3. New England
4. tired but it was a kind of tiredness all soft instead of sharp and mean
5. he loved the tastes, smells, gathering of the sap and the work itself
6. 40 degrees

Lesson 10
Fill in the Blanks
1. familiar
2. truant
3. suspicious
4. appetite
True and False
1. T
2. T
3. T
4. T
Multiple Choice
1. D
2. B
3. C
4. D
Who, What, Where, When, Why, and How
1. Marley's mother
2. the sugar camp
3. in that part of the country
4. she started asking questions about how to make maple sugar
5. it was the spring beauty and Chris didn't dream that anyone could find one already
6. the school bus is going to take them

Made in United States
Orlando, FL
23 July 2024